PIATTI

12 CAPRICES

Opus 25

FOR CELLO

Edited by PIERRE FOURNIER

Published in 2019 by Allegro Editions

12 Caprices for Cello
ISBN: 978-1-9748-9977-7 (paperback)

Cover design by Kaitlyn Whitaker

Cover image: "*Cello*" by Mindscape Studio courtesy of Shutterstock;
"*Music Sheet*" by danielo courtesy of Shutterstock

**ALLEGRO
EDITIONS**

12 CAPRICES
Opus 25, for Cello

Edited by PIERRE FOURNIER

ALFREDO PIATTI
(1822-1901)

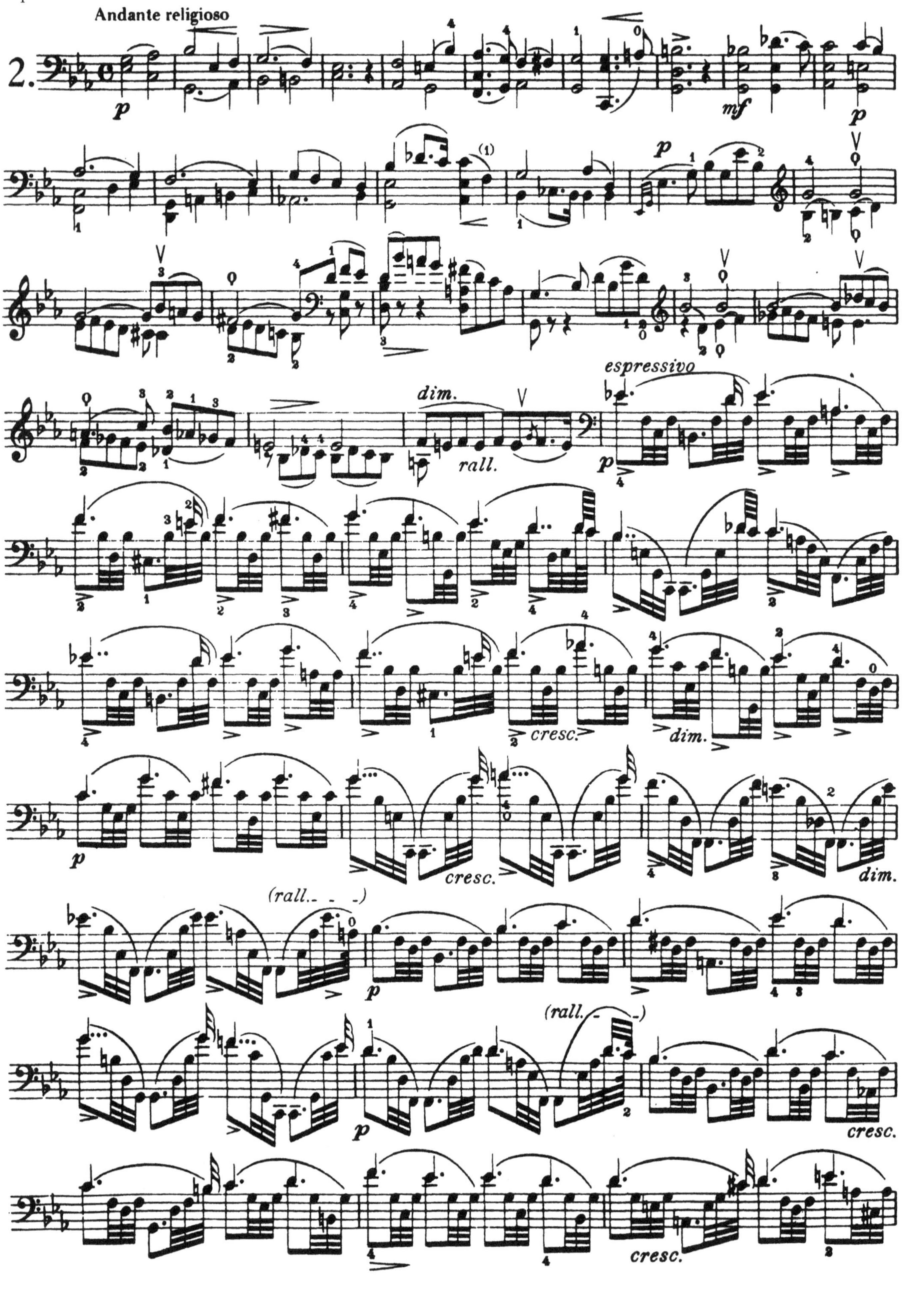
Andante religioso
2.
espressivo
dim.
rall.
cresc.
(rall.)

mf
dim.
rall.
p
in tempo
dim.
rall.
in Tempo
p
same position
mf
dim.
p
pp
ppp
pp

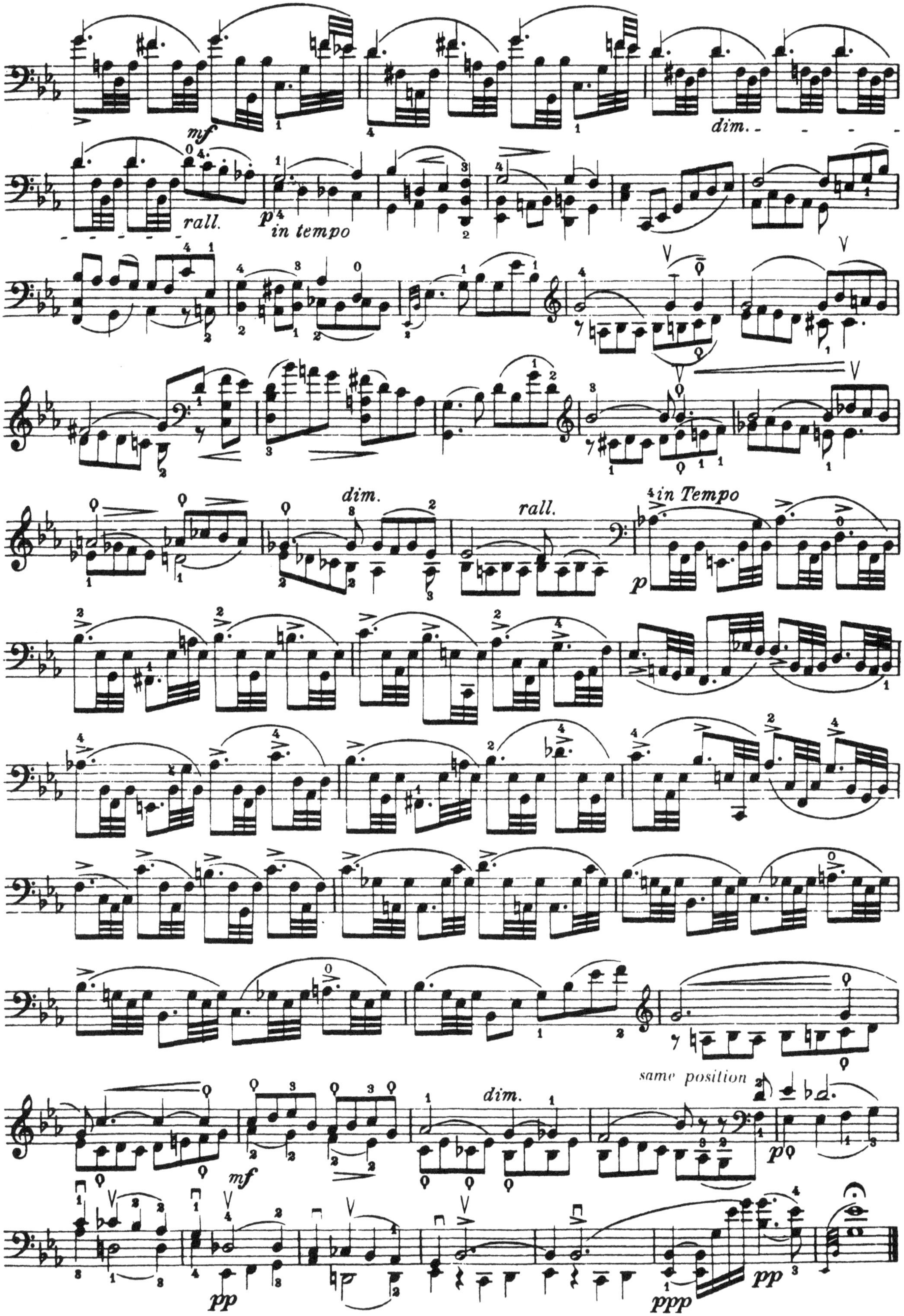

5. Allegro comodo

13

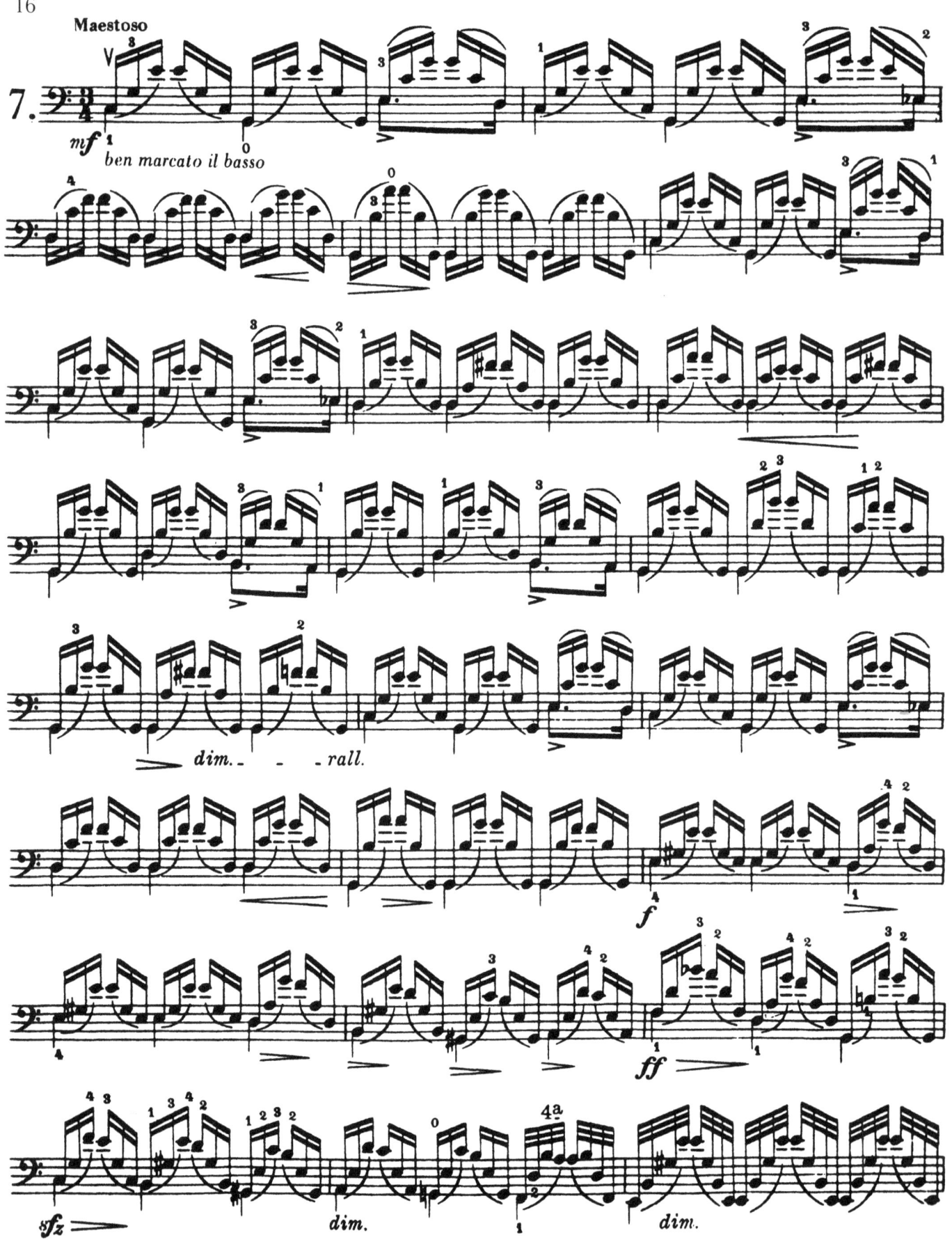

24

10. Allegro deciso

To be also practised with these 3 different bowings (except the last 6 measures)

1.   2.   3.

26

www.ingramcontent.com/pod-product-compliance
Lightning Source LLC
Chambersburg PA
CBHW081357040426
42451CB00017B/3481